D0831802

sed & awk
Pocket Reference

Arnold Robbins

Beijing • Cambridge • Farnham • Köln • Paris • Sebastopol • Taipei • Tokyo

sed & awk Pocket Reference

by Arnold Robbins

Copyright © 2000 O'Reilly & Associates, Inc. All rights reserved.
Printed in the United States of America. This material also appears
in *Unix in a Nutshell, Third Edition*, by Arnold Robbins, Copyright
© 1999, 1992, 1989 O'Reilly & Associates, Inc. Published by
O'Reilly & Associates, Inc., 101 Morris Street, Sebastopol, CA
95472.

Editor: Chuck Toporek

Production Editor: Jeffrey Liggett

Cover Design: Ellie Volckhausen

Printing History:

January 2000:   First Edition.

1-56592-729-X   [1/01]
[C]

Table of Contents

Introduction 1

Conventions 1

Matching Text 2

The sed Editor 11

The awk Programming Language 22

sed & awk Pocket Reference

Introduction

This pocket reference is a companion volume to O'Reilly's *sed & awk, Second Edition*, by Dale Dougherty and Arnold Robbins. It presents a concise summary of regular expressions and pattern matching, and summaries of sed and awk.

Conventions

The pocket reference follows certain typographic conventions, outlined here:

Constant Width
> Is used for code examples, commands, directory names, filenames, and options.

Constant Width Italic
> Is used in syntax and command summaries to show replaceable text; this text should be replaced with user-supplied values.

Constant Width Bold
> Is used in code examples to show commands or other text that should be typed literally by the user.

Italic
> Is used to show generic arguments and options; these should be replaced with user-supplied values. Italic is also used to highlight comments in examples.

$ Is used in some examples as the Bourne shell or Korn shell prompt.

[ ] Surround optional elements in a description of syntax. (The brackets themselves should never be typed.)

Matching Text

A number of Unix text-processing utilities let you search for, and in some cases change, text patterns rather than fixed strings. These utilities include the editing programs ed, ex, vi, and sed, the awk programming language, and the commands grep and egrep. Text patterns (formally called *regular expressions*) contain normal characters mixed with special characters (called *metacharacters*).

This section presents the following topics:

- Filenames versus patterns

- List of metacharacters available to each program

- Description of metacharacters

- Examples

Filenames Versus Patterns

Metacharacters used in pattern matching are different from metacharacters used for filename expansion. When you issue a command on the command line, special characters are seen first by the shell, then by the program; therefore, unquoted metacharacters are interpreted by the shell for filename expansion. The command:

```
$ grep [A-Z]* chap[12]
```

could, for example, be transformed by the shell into:

```
$ grep Array.c Bug.c Comp.c chap1 chap2
```

and would then try to find the pattern Array.c in files Bug.c, Comp.c, chap1, and chap2. To bypass the shell and pass the special characters to grep, use quotes:

```
$ grep "[A-Z]*" chap[12]
```

Double quotes suffice in most cases, but single quotes are the safest bet.

Note also that in pattern matching, ? matches zero or one instance of a regular expression; in filename expansion, ? matches a single character.

Metacharacters

Search patterns

The characters in the following table have special meaning only in search patterns:

Character	Pattern
.	Match any *single* character except newline. Can match newline in awk.
*	Match any number (or none) of the single character that immediately precedes it. The preceding character can also be a regular expression. E.g., since . (dot) means any character, .* means "match any number of any character."
^	Match the following regular expression at the beginning of the line or string.
$	Match the preceding regular expression at the end of the line or string.

Character	Pattern
[ ]	Match any *one* of the enclosed characters. A hyphen (-) indicates a range of consecutive characters. A circumflex (^) as the first character in the brackets reverses the sense: it matches any one character *not* in the list. A hyphen or close bracket (]) as the first character is treated as a member of the list. All other metacharacters are treated as members of the list (i.e., literally).
{n,m}	Match a range of occurrences of the single character that immediately precedes it. The preceding character can also be a metacharacter. {n} matches exactly *n* occurrences, {n,} matches at least *n* occurrences, and {n,m} matches any number of occurrences between *n* and *m*. *n* and *m* must be between 0 and 255, inclusive.
\{n,m\}	Just like {n,m}, earlier, but with backslashes in front of the braces.
\	Turn off the special meaning of the following character.
\(\)	Save the pattern enclosed between \(and \) into a special holding space. Up to nine patterns can be saved on a single line. The text matched by the subpatterns can be "replayed" in substitutions by the escape sequences \1 to \9.
\n	Replay the *n*th sub-pattern enclosed in \(and \) into the pattern at this point. *n* is a number from 1 to 9, with 1 starting on the left. See the following examples.
\< \>	Match characters at beginning (\<) or end (\>) of a word.
+	Match one or more instances of preceding regular expression.
?	Match zero or one instances of preceding regular expression.
|	Match the regular expression specified before or after.
( )	Apply a match to the enclosed group of regular expressions.

Many Unix systems allow the use of POSIX "character classes" within the square brackets that enclose a group of characters.

These are typed enclosed in [: and :]. For example, [[:alnum:]] matches a single alphanumeric character.

Class	Characters Matched
alnum	Alphanumeric characters
alpha	Alphabetic characters
blank	Space or tab
cntrl	Control characters
digit	Decimal digits
graph	Non-space characters
lower	Lowercase characters
print	Printable characters
space	White-space characters
upper	Uppercase characters
xdigit	Hexadecimal digits

Replacement patterns

The characters in the following table have special meaning only in replacement patterns.

Character	Pattern
\	Turn off the special meaning of the following character.
\n	Restore the text matched by the *n*th pattern previously saved by \(and \). *n* is a number from 1 to 9, with 1 starting on the left.
&	Reuse the text matched by the search pattern as part of the replacement pattern.
~	Reuse the previous replacement pattern in the current replacement pattern. Must be the only character in the replacement pattern. (ex and vi).

Character	Pattern
%	Reuse the previous replacement pattern in the current replacement pattern. Must be the only character in the replacement pattern. (ed).
\u	Convert first character of replacement pattern to uppercase.
\U	Convert entire replacement pattern to uppercase.
\l	Convert first character of replacement pattern to lowercase.
\L	Convert entire replacement pattern to lowercase.

Metacharacters, Listed by Unix Program

Some metacharacters are valid for one program but not for another. Those that are available to a Unix program are marked by a bullet (•) in the following table. (This table is correct for SVR4 and Solaris and most commerical Unix systems, but it's always a good idea to verify your system's behavior.) Items marked with a "P" are specified by POSIX; double check your system's version. Full descriptions were provided in the previous section.

Symbol	ed	vi/ex	sed/grep	awk/egrep	Action
.	•	•	•	•	Match any character.
*	•	•	•	•	Match zero or more preceding.
^	•	•	•	•	Match beginning of line/string.
$	•	•	•	•	Match end of line/string.
\	•	•	•	•	Escape following character.
[ ]	•	•	•	•	Match one from a set.
\(\)	•	•	•		Store pattern for later replay.[a]
\n	•	•	•		Replay sub-pattern in match.

Symbol	ed	vi/ ex	sed/ grep	awk/ egrep	Action
{ }				• P	Match a range of instances.
\{ \}	•	•	•		Match a range of instances.
\< \>	•	•			Match word's beginning/end.
+				•	Match one/more preceding.
?				•	Match zero/one preceding.
|				•	Separate choices to match.
( )				•	Group expressions to match.

a Stored sub-patterns can be "replayed" during matching. See the examples in the following table.

Note that in ed, ex, vi, and sed, you specify both a search pattern (on the left) and a replacement pattern (on the right). The metacharacters above are meaningful only in a search pattern.

In ed, ex, vi, and sed, the following metacharacters are valid only in a replacement pattern:

Symbol	ex	vi	sed	ed	Action
\	•	•	•	•	Escape following character.
\n	•	•	•	•	Text matching pattern stored in \(\).
&	•	•	•	•	Text matching search pattern.
~	•	•			Reuse previous replacement pattern.
%				•	Reuse previous replacement pattern.
\u \U	•	•			Change character(s) to uppercase.
\l \L	•	•			Change character(s) to lowercase.
\E	•	•			Turn off previous \U or \L.
\e	•	•			Turn off previous \u or \l.

Examples of Searching

When used with grep or egrep, regular expressions should be surrounded by quotes. (If the pattern contains a $, you must use single quotes; e.g., '*pattern*'.) When used with ed, ex, sed, and awk, regular expressions are usually surrounded by / although (except for awk), any delimiter works. Here are some example patterns.

Pattern	What Does It Match?
bag	The string *bag*.
^bag	*bag* at the beginning of the line.
bag$	*bag* at the end of the line.
^bag$	*bag* as the only word on the line.
[Bb]ag	*Bag* or *bag*.
b[aeiou]g	Second letter is a vowel.
b[^aeiou]g	Second letter is a consonant (or uppercase or symbol).
b.g	Second letter is any character.
^...$	Any line containing exactly three characters.
^\.	Any line that begins with a dot.
^\.[a-z][a-z]	Same, followed by two lowercase letters (e.g., troff requests).
^\.[a-z]\{2\}	Same as previous, ed, grep and sed only.
^[^.]	Any line that doesn't begin with a dot.
bugs*	*bug*, *bugs*, *bugss*, etc.
"word"	A word in quotes.
"*word"*	A word, with or without quotes.
[A-Z][A-Z]*	One or more uppercase letters.
[A-Z]+	Same as previous, egrep or awk only.
[[:upper:]]+	Same as previous, POSIX egrep or awk.
[A-Z].*	An uppercase letter, followed by zero or more characters.

Pattern	What Does It Match?
[A-Z]*	Zero or more uppercase letters.
[a-zA-Z]	Any letter, either lower- or uppercase.
[^0-9A-Za-z]	Any symbol or space (not a letter or a number).
[^[:alnum:]]	Same, using POSIX character class.

egrep or awk pattern	What Does It Match?
[567]	One of the numbers *5*, *6*, or *7*.
five|six|seven	One of the words *five*, *six*, or *seven*.
80[2-4]?86	*8086*, *80286*, *80386*, or *80486*.
80[2-4]?86|(Pentium(-II)?)	*8086*, *80286*, *80386*, *80486*, *Pentium*, or *Pentium-II*.
compan(y|ies)	*company* or *companies*.

ex or vi pattern	What Does It Match?
\<the	Words like *theater*, *there* or *the*.
the\>	Words like *breathe*, *seethe* or *the*.
\<the\>	The word *the*.

ed, sed, or grep pattern	What Does It Match?
0\{5,\}	Five or more zeros in a row.
[0-9]\{3\}-[0-9]\{2\}-[0-9]\{4\}	U.S. Social Security number (*nnn-nn-nnnn*).
\(why\).*\1	A line with two occurrences of *why*.
\([[:alpha:]_][[:alnum:]_.]*\) = \1;	C/C++ simple assignment statements.

Examples of searching and replacing

The following examples show the metacharacters available to sed or ex. Note that ex commands begin with a colon. A space is marked by a □; a tab is marked by a ➡.

Command	Result
s/.*/(&)/	Redo the entire line, but add parentheses.
s/.*/mv & &.old/	Change a wordlist (one word per line) into mv commands.
/^$/d	Delete blank lines.
:g/^$/d	Same as previous, in ex editor.
/^[□➡]*$/d	Delete blank lines, plus lines containing only spaces or tabs.
:g/^[□➡]*$/d	Same as previous, in ex editor.
s/□□*/□/g	Turn one or more spaces into one space.
:%s/□□*/□/g	Same as previous, in ex editor.
:s/[0-9]/Item &:/	Turn a number into an item label (on the current line).
:s	Repeat the substitution on the first occurrence.
:&	Same as previous.
:sg	Same as previous, but for all occurrences on the line.
:&g	Same as previous.
:%&g	Repeat the substitution globally (i.e., on all lines).
:.,$s/Fortran/\U&/g	On current line to last line, change word to uppercase.
:%s/.*/\L&/	Lowercase entire file.
:s/\<./\u&/g	Uppercase first letter of each word on current line. (Useful for titles.)
:%s/yes/No/g	Globally change a word to *No*.

Command	Result
`:%s/Yes/~/g`	Globally change a different word to *No* (previous replacement).

Finally, some `sed` examples for transposing words. A simple transposition of two words might look like this:

```
s/die or do/do or die/          Transpose words
```

The real trick is to use hold buffers to transpose variable patterns. For example:

```
s/\([Dd]ie\) or \([Dd]o\)/\2 or \1/   Transpose, using
                                       hold buffers
```

The sed Editor

This section presents the following topics:

- Conceptual overview of `sed`
- Command-line syntax
- Syntax of `sed` commands
- Group summary of `sed` commands
- Alphabetical summary of `sed` commands

Conceptual Overview

`sed` is a non-interactive, or stream-oriented, editor. It interprets a script and performs the actions in the script. `sed` is stream-oriented because, like many Unix programs, input flows through the program and is directed to standard output. For example, `sort` is stream-oriented; `vi` is not. `sed`'s input typically comes from a file or pipe, but it can also be directed

---

from the keyboard. Output goes to the screen by default but can be captured in a file or sent through a pipe instead.

The Free Software Foundation has a version of sed, available from *ftp://gnudist.gnu.org/gnu/sed/sed-3.02.tar.gz*. The somewhat older version, 2.05, is also available.

Typical uses of sed include:

- Editing one or more files automatically

- Simplifying repetitive edits to multiple files

- Writing conversion programs

sed operates as follows:

- Each line of input is copied into a "pattern space," an internal buffer where editing operations are performed.

- All editing commands in a sed script are applied, in order, to each line of input.

- Editing commands are applied to all lines (globally) unless line addressing restricts the lines affected.

- If a command changes the input, subsequent commands and address tests will be applied to the current line in the pattern space, not the original input line.

- The original input file is unchanged because the editing commands modify a copy of each original input line. The copy is sent to standard output (but can be redirected to a file).

- sed also maintains the "hold space," a separate buffer that can be used to save data for later retrieval.

Command-Line Syntax

The syntax for invoking sed has two forms:

```
sed [-n] [-e] 'command' file(s)
sed [-n]  -f  scriptfile file(s)
```

The first form allows you to specify an editing command on the command line, surrounded by single quotes. The second form allows you to specify a *scriptfile*, a file containing sed commands. Both forms may be used together, and they may be used multiple times. If no *file(s)* is specified, sed reads from standard input.

The following options are recognized:

-n   Suppress the default output; sed displays only those lines specified with the p command or with the p flag of the s command.

-e *cmd*
   Next argument is an editing command. Useful if multiple scripts or commands are specified.

-f *file*
   Next argument is a file containing editing commands.

If the first line of the script is #n, sed behaves as if -n had been specified.

Syntax of sed Commands

sed commands have the general form:

```
[address[,address]][!]command [arguments]
```

sed copies each line of input into the pattern space. sed instructions consist of *addresses* and editing *commands*. If the address of the command matches the line in the pattern

---

space, then the command is applied to that line. If a command has no address, then it is applied to each input line. If a command changes the contents of the pattern space, subsequent commands and addresses will be applied to the current line in the pattern space, not the original input line.

commands consist of a single letter or symbol; they are described later, alphabetically and by group. *arguments* include the label supplied to b or t, the filename supplied to r or w, and the substitution flags for s. *addresses* are described in the next section.

Pattern addressing

A sed command can specify zero, one, or two addresses. An address can be a line number, the symbol $ (for last line), or a regular expression enclosed in slashes (/*pattern*/). Regular expressions are described in "Matching Text." Additionally, \n can be used to match any newline in the pattern space (resulting from the N command), but not the newline at the end of the pattern space.

If the Command Specifies:	Then the Command Is Applied To:
No address	Each input line.
One address	Any line matching the address. Some commands accept only one address: a, i, r, q, and =.
Two comma-separated addresses	First matching line and all succeeding lines up to and including a line matching the second address.
An address followed by !	All lines that do *not* match the address.

Examples

`s/xx/yy/g`	Substitute on all lines (all occurrences).
`/BSD/d`	Delete lines containing BSD.
`/^BEGIN/,/^END/p`	Print between BEGIN and END, inclusive.
`/SAVE/!d`	Delete any line that doesn't contain SAVE.
`/BEGIN/,/END/!s/xx/yy/g`	Substitute on all lines, except between BEGIN and END.

Braces ({ }) are used in sed to nest one address inside another or to apply multiple commands at the same address.

```
[/pattern/[,/pattern/]]{
command1
command2
}
```

The opening curly brace must end its line, and the closing curly brace must be on a line by itself. Be sure there are no spaces after the braces.

Group Summary of sed Commands

In the lists that follow, the sed commands are grouped by function and are described tersely. Full descriptions, including syntax and examples, can be found afterward in the "Alphabetical Summary of sed Commands" section.

Basic editing

a\	Append text after a line.
c\	Replace text (usually a text block).
i\	Insert text before a line.
d	Delete lines.
s	Make substitutions.
y	Translate characters (like Unix tr).

Line information

=	Display line number of a line.
l	Display control characters in ASCII.
p	Display the line.

Input/output processing

n	Skip current line and go to line below.
r	Read another file's contents into the output stream.
w	Write input lines to another file.
q	Quit the sed script (no further output).

Yanking and putting

h	Copy into hold space; wipe out what's there.
H	Copy into hold space; append to what's there.
g	Get the hold space back; wipe out the destination line.
G	Get the hold space back; append to the pattern space.
x	Exchange contents of the hold and pattern spaces.

Branching commands

b   Branch to *label* or to end of script.

t   Same as b, but branch only after substitution.

`:label`   Label branched to by t or b.

Multiline input processing

N   Read another line of input (creates embedded newline).

D   Delete up to the embedded newline.

P   Print up to the embedded newline.

Alphabetical Summary of sed Commands

sed Command	Description
#	#
	Begin a comment in a sed script. Valid only as the first character of the first line. (Some versions allow comments anywhere, but it is better not to rely on this.) If the first line of the script is #n, sed behaves as if -n had been specified.
:	`:label`
	Label a line in the script for the transfer of control by b or t. *label* may contain up to seven characters.
=	`[/pattern/]=`
	Write to standard output the line number of each line addressed by *pattern*.
a	`[address]a\` `text`
	Append *text* following each line matched by *address*. If *text* goes over more than one line, newlines must

sed Command	Description
a	be "hidden" by preceding them with a backslash. The *text* will be terminated by the first newline that is not hidden in this way. The *text* is not available in the pattern space, and subsequent commands cannot be applied to it. The results of this command are sent to standard output when the list of editing commands is finished, regardless of what happens to the current line in the pattern space.
b	[*address1*[,*address2*]]b[*label*] Unconditionally transfer control to :*label* elsewhere in script. That is, the command following the *label* is the next command applied to the current line. If no *label* is specified, control falls through to the end of the script, so no more commands are applied to the current line.
c	[*address1*[,*address2*]]c\\ *text* Replace (change) the lines selected by the address(es) with *text*. (See a for details on *text*.) When a range of lines is specified, all lines are replaced as a group by a single copy of *text*. The contents of the pattern space are, in effect, deleted and no subsequent editing commands can be applied to the pattern space (or to *text*).
d	[*address1*[,*address2*]]d Delete the addressed line (or lines) from the pattern space. Thus, the line is not passed to standard output. A new line of input is read, and editing resumes with the first command in the script.
D	[*address1*[,*address2*]]D Delete the first part (up to embedded newline) of multi-line pattern space created by N command and resume editing with first command in script. If this

sed Command	Description
D	command empties the pattern space, then a new line of input is read, as if the d command had been executed.
g	[address1[,address2]]g Paste the contents of the hold space (see **h** and **H**) back into the pattern space, wiping out the previous contents of the pattern space.
G	[address1[,address2]]G Same as g, except that a newline and the hold space are pasted to the end of the pattern space instead of overwriting it.
h	[address1[,address2]]h Copy the pattern space into the hold space, a special temporary buffer. The previous contents of the hold space are obliterated. You can use h to save a line before editing it.
H	[address1[,address2]]H Append a newline and then the contents of the pattern space to the contents of the hold space. Even if the hold space is empty, H still appends a newline. H is like an incremental copy.
i	[address1]i\ text Insert *text* before each line matched by *address*. (See **a** for details on *text*.)
l	[address1[,address2]]l List the contents of the pattern space, showing non-printing characters as ASCII codes. Long lines are wrapped.

sed Command	Description
n	[address1[,address2]]n
	Read the next line of input into pattern space. The current line is sent to standard output, and the next line becomes the current line. Control passes to the command following n instead of resuming at the top of the script.
N	[address1[,address2]]N
	Append the next input line to contents of pattern space; the new line is separated from the previous contents of the pattern space by a newline. (This command is designed to allow pattern matches across two lines.) By using \n to match the embedded newline, you can match patterns across multiple lines.
p	[address1[,address2]]p
	Print the addressed line(s). Note that this can result in duplicate output unless default output is suppressed by using #n or the -n command-line option. Typically used before commands that change flow control (d, n, b), which might prevent the current line from being output.
P	[address1[,address2]]P
	Print first part (up to embedded newline) of multiline pattern space created by N command. Same as p if N has not been applied to a line.
q	[address]q
	Quit when *address* is encountered. The addressed line is first written to the output (if default output is not suppressed), along with any text appended to it by previous a or r commands.
r	[address]r file
	Read contents of *file* and append after the contents of the pattern space. There must be exactly one space between the r and the filename.

sed Command	Description
s	[*address1*[,*address2*]]s/*pat*/*repl*/[*flags*]
	Substitute *repl* for *pat* on each addressed line. If pattern addresses are used, the pattern // represents the last pattern address specified. Any delimiter may be used. Use \ within *pat* or *repl* to escape the delimiter. The following flags can be specified:
	n Replace *n*th instance of *pat* on each addressed line. *n* is any number in the range 1 to 512; the default is 1.
	g Replace all instances of *pat* on each addressed line, not just the first instance.
	p Print the line if the substitution is successful. If several substitutions are successful, sed will print multiple copies of the line.
	w *file* Write the line to *file* if a replacement was done. A maximum of 10 different *files* can be opened.
t	[*address1*[,*address2*]]t [*label*]
	Test if successful substitutions have been made on addressed lines, and if so, branch to the line marked by :*label*. (See b and :.) If *label* is not specified, control branches to the bottom of the script. The t command is like a case statement in the C programming language or the various shell programming languages. You test each case; when it's true, you exit the construct.
w	[*address1*[,*address2*]]w *file*
	Append contents of pattern space to *file*. This action occurs when the command is encountered rather than when the pattern space is output. Exactly one space must separate the w and the filename. A maximum of 10 different files can be opened in a script. This command will create the file if it does not exist; if the file

sed Command	Description
w	exists, its contents will be overwritten each time the script is executed. Multiple write commands that direct output to the same file append to the end of the file.
x	[*address1*[,*address2*]]x Exchange the contents of the pattern space with the contents of the hold space.
y	[*address1*[,*address2*]]y/*abc*/*xyz*/ Translate characters. Change every instance of *a* to *x*, *b* to *y*, *c* to *z*, etc.

The awk Programming Language

This section presents the following topics:

- Conceptual overview
- Command-line syntax
- Patterns and procedures
- Built-in variables
- Operators
- Variables and array assignment
- User-defined functions
- Group listing of functions and commands
- Implementation limits
- Alphabetical summary of functions and commands

Conceptual Overview

awk is a pattern-matching program for processing files, especially when they are databases. The new version of awk, called nawk, provides additional capabilities. (It really isn't so new. The additional features were added in 1984, and it was first shipped with System V Release 3.1 in 1987. Nevertheless, the name was never changed on most systems.) Every modern Unix system comes with a version of new awk, and its use is recommended over old awk.

Different systems vary in what the two versions are called. Some have oawk and awk, for the old and new versions, respectively. Others have awk and nawk. Still others only have awk, which is the new version. This example shows what happens if your awk is the old one:

```
$ awk 1 /dev/null
awk: syntax error near line 1
awk: bailing out near line 1
```

awk will exit silently if it is the new version.

Source code for the latest version of awk, from Bell Labs, can be downloaded starting at Brian Kernighan's home page: *http://cm.bell-labs.com/~bwk*. Michael Brennan's mawk is available via anonymous FTP from *ftp://ftp.whidbey.net/pub/brennan/mawk1.3.3.tar.gz*. Finally, the Free Software Foundation has a version of awk called gawk, available from *ftp://gnudist.gnu.org/gnu/gawk/gawk-3.0.4.tar.gz*. All three programs implement "new" awk. Thus, references in the following text such as "nawk only," apply to all three. gawk has additional features.

With original awk, you can:

• Think of a text file as made up of records and fields in a textual database.

- Perform arithmetic and string operations.

- Use programming constructs such as loops and conditionals.

- Produce formatted reports.

With nawk, you can also:

- Define your own functions.

- Execute Unix commands from a script.

- Process the results of Unix commands.

- Process command-line arguments more gracefully.

- Work more easily with multiple input streams.

- Flush open output files and pipes (latest Bell Labs awk).

In addition, with GNU awk (gawk), you can:

- Use regular expressions to separate records, as well as fields.

- Skip to the start of the next file, not just the next record.

- Perform more powerful string substitutions.

- Retrieve and format system time values.

Command-Line Syntax

The syntax for invoking awk has two forms:

```
awk [options] 'script' var=value file(s)
awk [options] -f scriptfile var=value file(s)
```

You can specify a *script* directly on the command line, or you can store a script in a *scriptfile* and specify it with -f. nawk

---

allows multiple -f scripts. Variables can be assigned a value on the command line. The value can be a literal, a shell variable ($name), or a command substitution (`cmd`), but the value is available only after the BEGIN statement is executed.

awk operates on one or more *files*. If none are specified (or if - is specified), awk reads from the standard input.

The recognized options are:

-F*fs*

> Set the field separator to *fs*. This is the same as setting the built-in variable FS. Original awk only allows the field separator to be a single character. nawk allows *fs* to be a regular expression. Each input line, or record, is divided into fields by white space (spaces or tabs) or by some other user-definable field separator. Fields are referred to by the variables $1, $2,..., $*n*. $0 refers to the entire record.

-v *var=value*

> Available in nawk only. Assign a *value* to variable *var*. This allows assignment before the script begins execution.

For example, to print the first three (colon-separated) fields of each record on separate lines:

```
awk -F: '{ print $1; print $2; print $3 }' /etc/passwd
```

Numerous examples are shown later in the "Simple pattern-procedure examples" section.

Patterns and Procedures

awk scripts consist of patterns and procedures:

```
pattern   { procedure }
```

Both are optional. If *pattern* is missing, { *procedure* } is applied to all lines. If { *procedure* } is missing, the matched line is printed.

Patterns

A pattern can be any of the following:

```
/regular expression/
relational expression
pattern-matching expression
BEGIN
END
```

- Expressions can be composed of quoted strings, numbers, operators, functions, defined variables, or any of the predefined variables described later under "Built-in Variables."

- Regular expressions use the extended set of metacharacters and are described earlier in "Matching Text."

- ^ and $ refer to the beginning and end of a string (such as the fields), respectively, rather than the beginning and end of a line. In particular, these metacharacters will *not* match at a newline embedded in the middle of a string.

- Relational expressions use the relational operators listed under "Operators" later in this book. For example, $2 > $1 selects lines for which the second field is greater than the first. Comparisons can be either string or numeric. Thus, depending on the types of data in $1 and $2, awk will do either a numeric or a string comparison. This can change from one record to the next.

- Pattern-matching expressions use the operators ~ (match) and !~ (don't match). See "Operators" later in this book.

- The BEGIN pattern lets you specify procedures that will take place *before* the first input line is processed. (Generally, you set global variables here.)

- The END pattern lets you specify procedures that will take place *after* the last input record is read.

- In nawk, BEGIN and END patterns may appear multiple times. The procedures are merged as if there had been one large procedure.

Except for BEGIN and END, patterns can be combined with the Boolean operators || (or), && (and), and ! (not). A range of lines can also be specified using comma-separated patterns:

```
pattern,pattern
```

Procedures

Procedures consist of one or more commands, functions, or variable assignments, separated by newlines or semicolons, and are contained within curly braces. Commands fall into five groups:

- Variable or array assignments
- Printing commands
- Built-in functions
- Control-flow commands
- User-defined functions (nawk only)

Simple pattern-procedure examples

Print first field of each line:

```
{ print $1 }
```

Print all lines that contain *pattern*:

```
/pattern/
```

Print first field of lines that contain *pattern*:

```
/pattern/ { print $1 }
```

Select records containing more than two fields:

```
NF > 2
```

Interpret input records as a group of lines up to a blank line. Each line is a single field:

```
BEGIN { FS = "\n"; RS = "" }
```

Print fields 2 and 3 in switched order, but only on lines whose first field matches the string URGENT:

```
$1 ~ /URGENT/ { print $3, $2 }
```

Count and print the number of *pattern* found:

```
/pattern/ { ++x }
END { print x }
```

Add numbers in second column and print total:

```
{ total += $2 }
END { print "column total is", total}
```

Print lines that contain less than 20 characters:

```
length($0) < 20
```

Print each line that begins with *Name:* and that contains exactly seven fields:

```
NF == 7 && /^Name:/
```

Print the fields of each record in reverse order, one per line:

```
    {
            for (I - NF, i >= 1; i   )
                    print $i
    }
```

Built-in Variables

All awk variables are included in nawk. All nawk variables are included in gawk.

Version	Variable	Description
awk	FILENAME	Current filename.
	FS	Field separator (a space).
	NF	Number of fields in current record.
	NR	Number of the current record.
	OFMT	Output format for numbers ("%.6g") and for conversion to string.
	OFS	Output field separator (a space).
	ORS	Output record separator (a newline).
	RS	Record separator (a newline).
	$0	Entire input record.
	$n	nth field in current record; fields are separated by FS.
nawk	ARGC	Number of arguments on the command line.
	ARGV	An array containing the command-line arguments, indexed from 0 to ARGC $-$ 1.
	CONVFMT	String conversion format for numbers ("%.6g"). (POSIX)
	ENVIRON	An associative array of environment variables.
	FNR	Like NR, but relative to the current file.

Version	Variable	Description
nawk	RLENGTH	Length of the string matched by match( ) function.
	RSTART	First position in the string matched by match( ) function.
	SUBSEP	Separator character for array subscripts ("\034").
gawk	ARGIND	Index in ARGV of current input file.
	ERRNO	A string indicating the error when a redirection fails for getline or if close( ) fails.
	FIELDWIDTHS	A space-separated list of field widths to use for splitting up the record, instead of FS.
	IGNORECASE	When true, all regular expression matches, string comparisons and index( ) ignore case.
	RT	The text matched by RS, which can be a regular expression in gawk.

Operators

The following table lists the operators, in order of increasing precedence, that are available in awk.

Symbol	Meaning
= += −= *= /= %= ^= **=	Assignment.
?:	C conditional expression (nawk only).
||	Logical OR (short-circuit).
&&	Logical AND (short-circuit).
in	Array membership (nawk only).
~ !~	Match regular expression and negation.
< <= > >= != ==	Relational operators.
(blank)	Concatenation.
+ -	Addition, subtraction.

Symbol	Meaning
* / %	Multiplication, division, and modulus (remainder).
+ - !	Unary plus and minus, and logical negation.
^ **	Exponentiation.
++ - -	Increment and decrement, either prefix or postfix.
$	Field reference.

Note: While ** and **= are common extensions, they are not part of POSIX awk.

Variables and Array Assignments

Variables can be assigned a value with an = sign. For example:

```
FS = ","
```

Expressions using the operators +, -, /, and % (modulo) can be assigned to variables.

Arrays can be created with the split() function (described later), or they can simply be named in an assignment statement. Array elements can be subscripted with numbers (*array*[1], ..., *array*[*n*]) or with strings. Arrays subscripted by strings are called "associative arrays." (In fact, all arrays in awk are associative; numeric subscripts are converted to strings before using them as array subscripts. Associative arrays are one of awk's most powerful features.)

For example, to count the number of widgets you have, you could use the following script:

```
/widget/ { count["widget"]++ }          Count widgets
END      { print count["widget"] }       Print the count
```

You can use the special `for` loop to read all the elements of an associative array:

```
for (item in array)
        process array[item]
```

The index of the array is available as `item`, while the value of an element of the array can be referenced as `array[item]`.

You can use the operator `in` to test that an element exists by testing to see if its index exists (nawk only). For example:

```
if (index in array)
        ...
```

tests that `array[index]` exists, but you cannot use it to test the value of the element referenced by `array[index]`.

You can also delete individual elements of the array using the `delete` statement (nawk only).

Escape sequences

Within string and regular expression constants, the following escape sequences may be used.

Sequence	Meaning	Sequence	Meaning
\a	Alert (bell)	\v	Vertical tab
\b	Backspace	\\	Literal backslash
\f	Form feed	\nnn	Octal value nnn
\n	Newline	\xnn	Hexadecimal value nn
\r	Carriage return	\"	Literal double quote (in strings)
\t	Tab	\/	Literal slash (in regular expressions)

Note: The \x escape sequence is a common extension; it is not part of POSIX awk.

User-Defined Functions

nawk allows you to define your own functions. This makes it easy to encapsulate sequences of steps that need to be repeated into a single place, and re-use the code from anywhere in your program.

The following function capitalizes each word in a string. It has one parameter, named input, and five local variables, which are written as extra parameters:

```
# capitalize each word in a string
function capitalize(input,    result, words, n, i, w)
{
    result = ""
    n = split(input, words, " ")
    for (i = 1; i <= n; i++) {
        w = words[i]
        w = toupper(substr(w, 1, 1)) substr(w, 2)
        if (i > 1)
                result = result " "
        result = result w
    }
    return result
}

# main program, for testing
{ print capitalize($0) }
```

With this input data:

```
A test line with words and numbers like 12 on it.
```

This program produces:

```
A Test Line With Words And Numbers Like 12 On It.
```

Note: For user-defined functions, no space is allowed between the function name and the left parenthesis when the function is called.

Group Listing of awk Functions and Commands

awk functions and commands may be classified as follows:

Functions	Commands		
Arithmetic Functions	atan2[a]	int	sin[a]
	cos[a]	log	sqrt
	exp	rand[a]	srand[a]
String Functions	index	match[a]	tolower[a]
	gensub[b]	split	toupper[a]
	gsub[a]	sprintf	
	length	sub[a]	
Control Flow Statements	break	exit	return[a]
	continue	for	while
	do/while[a]	if	
Input/Output Processing	close[a]	next	printf
	fflush[c]	nextfile[c]	
	getline[a]	print	
Time Functions	strftime[b]	systime[b]	
Programming	delete[a]	function[a]	system[a]

[a] Available in nawk.

[b] Available in gawk.

[c] Available in Bell Labs awk and gawk.

Implementation Limits

Many versions of awk have various implementation limits, on things such as:

- Number of fields per record

- Number of characters per input record

- Number of characters per output record

- Number of characters per field

- Number of characters per `printf` string

- Number of characters in literal string

- Number of characters in character class

- Number of files open

- Number of pipes open

- The ability to handle 8-bit characters and characters that are all zero (ASCII NUL)

gawk does not have limits on any of the above items, other than those imposed by the machine architecture and/or the operating system.

Alphabetical Summary of Functions and Commands

The following alphabetical list of keywords and functions includes all that are available in awk, nawk, and gawk. nawk includes all old awk functions and keywords, plus some additional ones (marked as {N}). gawk includes all nawk functions and keywords, plus some additional ones (marked as {G}). Items marked with {B} are available in the Bell Labs awk. Items that aren't marked with a symbol are available in all versions.

Command	Description
atan2	`atan2(y, x)`
	Return the arctangent of y/x in radians. {N}
break	`break`
	Exit from a `while`, `for`, or `do` loop.
close	`close(expr)`
	In most implementations of `awk`, you can only have up to ten files open simultaneously and one pipe. Therefore, `nawk` provides a `close` function that allows you to close a file or a pipe. It takes the same expression that opened the pipe or file as an argument. This expression must be identical, character by character, to the one that opened the file or pipe—even whitespace is significant. {N}
continue	`continue`
	Begin next iteration of `while`, `for`, or `do` loop.
cos	`cos(x)`
	Return the cosine of x, an angle in radians. {N}
delete	`delete array[element]`
	`delete array`
	Delete *element* from *array*. The brackets are typed literally. {N}
	The second form is a common extension, which deletes *all* elements of the array at one shot. {B} {G}
do	`do`
	`statement`
	`while (expr)`
	Looping statement. Execute *statement*, then evaluate *expr* and if true, execute *statement* again. A series of statements must be put within braces. {N}

Command	Description
exit	exit [*expr*] Exit from script, reading no new input. The END procedure, if it exists, will be executed. An optional *expr* becomes awk's return value.
exp	exp(*x*) Return exponential of x (e^x).
fflush	fflush([*output-expr*]) Flush any buffers associated with open output file or pipe *output-expr*. {B} gawk extends this function. If no *output-expr* is supplied, it flushes standard output. If *output-expr* is the null string (" "), it flushes all open files and pipes. {G}
for	for (*init-expr*; *test-expr*; *incr-expr*) *statement* C-style looping construct. *init-expr* assigns the initial value of a counter variable. *test-expr* is a relational expression that is evaluated each time before executing the *statement*. When *test-expr* is false, the loop is exited. *incr-expr* is used to increment the counter variable after each pass. All of the expressions are optional. A missing *test-expr* is considered to be true. A series of statements must be put within braces.
for	for (*item* in *array*) *statement* Special loop designed for reading associative arrays. For each element of the array, the *statement* is executed; the element can be referenced by *array*[*item*]. A series of statements must be put within braces.

Command	Description

function	`function name(parameter-list) {`
	    `statements`
	`}`
	
	Create *name* as a user-defined function consisting of awk *statements* that apply to the specified list of parameters. No space is allowed between *name* and the left parenthesis when the function is called. {N}

getline	`getline [var] [< file]` `command	getline [var]` Read next line of input. Original awk does not support the syntax to open multiple input streams. The first form reads input from *file* and the second form reads the output of *command*. Both forms read one record at a time, and each time the statement is executed it gets the next record of input. The record is assigned to $0 and is parsed into fields, setting NF, NR and FNR. If *var* is specified, the result is assigned to *var* and $0 and NF are not changed. Thus, if the result is assigned to a variable, the current record does not change. getline is actually a function and it returns 1 if it reads a record successfully, 0 if end-of-file is encountered, and −1 if for some reason it is otherwise unsuccessful. {N}
gensub	`gensub(r, s, h [, t])` General substitution function. Substitute *s* for matches of the regular expression *r* in the string *t*. If *h* is a number, replace the *h*th match. If it is "g" or "G", substitute globally. If *t* is not supplied, $0 is used. Return the new string value. The original *t* is *not* modified. (Compare **gsub** and **sub**.) {G}
gsub	`gsub(r, s [, t])` Globally substitute *s* for each match of the regular expression *r* in the string *t*. If *t* is not supplied, defaults to $0. Return the number of substitutions. {N}

Command	Description

if	```if (condition)```
	    ```statement```
	```[else```
	    ```statement]```
	
	If *condition* is true, do *statement(s)*, otherwise do *statement* in optional `else` clause. Condition can be an expression using any of the relational operators <, <=, ==, !=, >=, or >, as well as the array membership operator `in`, and the pattern-matching operators ~ and !~ (e.g., `if ($1 ~ /[Aa].*/`)). A series of statements must be put within braces. Another `if` can directly follow an `else` in order to produce a chain of tests or decisions.

index	```index(str, substr)``` Return the position (starting at 1) of *substr* in *str*, or zero if *substr* is not present in *str*.
int	```int(x)``` Return integer value of x by truncating any fractional part.
length	```length([arg])``` Return length of *arg*, or the length of $0 if no argument.
log	```log(x)``` Return the natural logarithm (base *e*) of x.
match	```match(s, r)``` Function that matches the pattern, specified by the regular expression *r*, in the string *s* and returns either the position in *s* where the match begins, or 0 if no occurrences are found. Sets the values of RSTART and RLENGTH to the start and length of the match, respectively. {N}
next	```next``` Read next input line and start new cycle through pattern/procedures statements.

Command	Description
nextfile	`nextfile`
	Stop processing the current input file and start new cycle through pattern/procedures statements, beginning with the first record of the next file. {B} {G}
print	`print [ output-expr[, ...]] [ dest-expr ]`
	Evaluate the *output-expr* and direct it to standard output followed by the value of ORS. Each comma-separated *output-expr* is separated in the output by the value of OFS. With no *output-expr*, print $0. The output may be redirected to a file or pipe via the *dest-expr*, which is described in the section "Output Redirections" following this table.
printf	`printf(format [, expr-list ]) [ dest-expr ]`
	An alternative output statement borrowed from the C language. It has the ability to produce formatted output. It can also be used to output data without automatically producing a newline. *format* is a string of format specifications and constants. *expr-list* is a list of arguments corresponding to format specifiers. As for print, output may be redirected to a file or pipe. See the section "printf formats" following this table for a description of allowed format specifiers.
rand	`rand()`
	Generate a random number between 0 and 1. This function returns the same series of numbers each time the script is executed, unless the random number generator is seeded using srand(). {N}
return	`return [expr]`
	Used within a user-defined function to exit the function, returning value of expression. The return value of a function is undefined if *expr* is not provided. {N}
sin	`sin(x)`
	Return the sine of *x*, an angle in radians. {N}

Command	Description
split	`split(string, array [, sep])` Split *string* into elements of array `array[1], ,array[n]`. The string is split at each occurrence of separator *sep*. If *sep* is not specified, FS is used. Returns the number of array elements created.
sprintf	`sprintf(format [, expressions])` Return the formatted value of one or more *expressions*, using the specified *format*. Data is formatted but not printed. See the section "printf formats" following this table for a description of allowed format specifiers.
sqrt	`sqrt(arg)` Return square root of *arg*.
srand	`srand([expr])` Use optional *expr* to set a new seed for the random number generator. Default is the time of day. Return value is the old seed. {N}
strftime	`strftime([format [,timestamp]])` Format *timestamp* according to *format*. Return the formatted string. The *timestamp* is a time-of-day value in seconds since Midnight, January 1, 1970, UTC. The *format* string is similar to that of `sprintf`. If *timestamp* is omitted, it defaults to the current time. If *format* is omitted, it defaults to a value that produces output similar to that of the Unix date command. {G}
sub	`sub(r, s [, t])` Substitute *s* for first match of the regular expression *r* in the string *t*. If *t* is not supplied, defaults to $0. Return 1 if successful; 0 otherwise. {N}
substr	`substr(string, beg [, len])` Return substring of *string* at beginning position *beg*, and the characters that follow to maximum specified length *len*. If no length is given, use the rest of the string.

Command	Description
system	`system(command)` Function that executes the specified *command* and returns its status. The status of the executed command typically indicates success or failure. A value of 0 means that the command executed successfully. A non-zero value indicates a failure of some sort. The documentation for the command you're running will give you the details. The output of the command is *not* available for processing within the awk script. Use *command* | `getline` to read the output of a command into the script. {N}
systime	`systime()` Return a time-of-day value in seconds since Midnight, January 1, 1970, UTC. {G}
tolower	`tolower(str)` Translate all uppercase characters in *str* to lowercase and return the new string.[a] {N}
toupper	`toupper(str)` Translate all lowercase characters in *str* to uppercase and return the new string. {N}

while	`while (condition)`
	　　`statement`
	
	Do *statement* while *condition* is true (see if for a description of allowable conditions). A series of statements must be put within braces.

[a] Very early versions of nawk don't support `tolower()` and `toupper()`. However, they are now part of the POSIX specification for awk.

Output redirections

For `print` and `printf`, *dest-expr* is an optional expression that directs the output to a file or pipe.

`> file`
> Directs the output to a file, overwriting its previous contents.

`>> file`
> Appends the output to a file, preserving its previous contents. In both of these cases, the file will be created if it does not already exist.

`| command`
> Directs the output as the input to a system command.

Be careful not to mix > and >> for the same file. Once a file has been opened with >, subsequent output statements continue to append to the file until it is closed.

Remember to call `close()` when you have finished with a file or pipe. If you don't, eventually you will hit the system limit on the number of simultaneously open files.

printf formats

Format specifiers for `printf` and `sprintf` have the following form:

```
%[flag][width][.precision]letter
```

The control letter is required. The format conversion control letters are given in the following table.

Character	Description
c	ASCII character.
d	Decimal integer.
i	Decimal integer. (Added in POSIX)
e	Floating-point format ([-]d.precisione[+-]dd).
E	Floating-point format ([-]d.precisionE[+-]dd).
f	Floating-point format ([-]ddd.precision).
g	e or f conversion, whichever is shortest, with trailing zeros removed.
G	E or f conversion, whichever is shortest, with trailing zeros removed.
o	Unsigned octal value.
u	Unsigned decimal value.
s	String.
x	Unsigned hexadecimal number. Uses a-f for 10 to 15.
X	Unsigned hexadecimal number. Uses A-F for 10 to 15.
%	Literal %.

The optional *flag* is one of the following:

Character	Description
-	Left-justify the formatted value within the field.
space	Prefix positive values with a space and negative values with a minus.
+	Always prefix numeric values with a sign, even if the value is positive.
#	Use an alternate form: %o has a preceding 0; %x and %X are prefixed with 0x and 0X, respectively; %e, %E and %f always have a decimal point in the result; and %g and %G do not have trailing zeros removed.
0	Pad output with zeros, not spaces. This only happens when the field width is wider than the converted result.

The optional *width* is the minimum number of characters to output. The result will be padded to this size if it is smaller. The 0 flag causes padding with zeros; otherwise, padding is with spaces.

The *precision* is optional. Its meaning varies by control letter, as shown in this table:

Conversion	Precision Means
%d, %i, %o, %u, %x, %X	The minimum number of digits to print.
%e, %E, %f	The number of digits to the right of the decimal point.
%g, %G	The maximum number of significant digits.
%s	The maximum number of characters to print.

More Titles from O'Reilly

In a Nutshell Quick References

Perl in a Nutshell

By Ellen Siever, Stephen Spainhour &
Nathan Patwardhan
1st Edition December 1998
674 pages, ISBN 1-56592-286-7

SCO UNIX in a Nutshell

By Ellie Cutler &
the Staff of O'Reilly & Associates
1st Edition February 1994
590 pages, ISBN 1-56592-037-6

Tcl/Tk in a Nutshell

By Paul Raines & Jeff Tranter
1st Edition March 1999
456 pages, ISBN 1-56592-433-9

UML in a Nutshell

By Sinan Si Albir
1st Edition September 1998
290 pages, ISBN 1-56592-448-7

UNIX in a Nutshell:
System V Edition, 3rd Edition

By Arnold Robbins
3rd Edition September 1999
616 pages, ISBN 1-56592-427-4

Year 2000 in a Nutshell

By Norman Shakespeare
1st Edition September 1998
330 pages, ISBN 1-56592-421-5

UNIX Basics

Learning the UNIX Operating
System, 4th Edition

By Jerry Peek, Grace Todino & John Strang
4th Edition December 1997
106 pages, ISBN 1-56592-390-1

Learning the vi Editor, 6th Edition

By Linda Lamb & Arnold Robbins
6th Edition November 1998
348 pages, ISBN 1-56592-426-6

Learning GNU Emacs, 2nd Edition

By Debra Cameron, Bill Rosenblatt &
Eric Raymond
2nd Edition September 1996
560 pages, ISBN 1-56592-152-6

Learning the Korn Shell

By Bill Rosenblatt
1st Edition June 1993
363 pages, ISBN 1-56592-054-6

O'REILLY

TO ORDER: **800-998-9938** • **order@oreilly.com** • **http://www.oreilly.com/**

OUR PRODUCTS ARE AVAILABLE AT A BOOKSTORE OR SOFTWARE STORE NEAR YOU.

FOR INFORMATION: **800-998-9938** • **707-829-0515** • **info@oreilly.com**

UNIX Basics

Using csh & tcsh
By Paul DuBois
1st Edition August 1995
242 pages, ISBN 1-56592-132-1

Volume 3M: X Window System User's Guide, Motif Edition
By Valerie Quercia & Tim O'Reilly
2nd Edition January 1993
956 pages, ISBN 1-56592-015-5

Perl

Learning Perl, 2nd Edition
By Randal L. Schwartz & Tom Christiansen
Foreword by Larry Wall
2nd Edition July 1997
302 pages, ISBN 1-56592-284-0

Learning Perl/Tk
By Nancy Walsh
1st Edition January 1999
376 pages, ISBN 1-56592-314-6

Learning Perl on Win32 Systems
By Randal L. Schwartz, Erik Olson &
Tom Christiansen
1st Edition August 1997
306 pages, ISBN 1-56592-324-3

Perl Cookbook
By Tom Christiansen & Nathan Torkington
1st Edition August 1998
794 pages, ISBN 1-56592-243-3

UNIX Tools

The UNIX CD Bookshelf
By O'Reilly & Associates, Inc.
1st Edition November 1998
444 pages, Features CD-ROM
ISBN 1-56592-406-1

lex & yacc, 2nd Edition
By John Levine, Tony Mason & Doug Brown
2nd Edition October 1992
366 pages, ISBN 1-56592-000-7

sed & awk, 2nd Edition
By Dale Dougherty & Arnold Robbins
2nd Edition March 1997
432 pages, ISBN 1-56592-225-5

Managing Projects with make, 2nd Edition
By Andrew Oram & Steve Talbott
2nd Edition October 1991
152 pages, ISBN 0-937175-90-0

UNIX Tools

Writing GNU Emacs Extensions

By Bob Glickstein
1st Edition April 1997
236 pages, ISBN 1-56592-261-1

UNIX Power Tools, 2nd Edition

By Jerry Peek, Tim O'Reilly & Mike Loukides
2nd Edition August 1997
1120 pages, Includes CD-ROM
ISBN 1-56592-260-3

Mastering Algorithms with Perl

By Jon Orwant, Jarkko Hietaniemi &
John Macdonald
1st Edition August 1999
704 pages, ISBN 1-56592-398-7

Programming Perl, 2nd Edition

By Larry Wall, Tom Christiansen &
Randal L. Schwartz
2nd Edition September 1996
670 pages, ISBN 1-56592-149-6

Advanced Perl Programming

By Sriram Srinivasan
1st Edition August 1997
434 pages, ISBN 1-56592-220-4

The Perl CD Bookshelf

By O'Reilly & Associates, Inc.
1st Edition July 1999
Features CD-ROM
ISBN 1-56592-462-2

CGI Programming with Perl, 2nd Edition

By Shishir Gundavaram
2nd Edition June 2000 (est.)
450 pages (est.), ISBN 1-56592-419-3